NOW
&
NOT
YET

NOW & NOT YET

JOHN BRUNT

REVIEW AND HERALD PUBLISHING ASSOCIATION
Washington, DC 20039-0555
Hagerstown, MD 21740

This book was
Edited by Richard W. Coffen
Designed by Richard Steadham
Type set:11/12 Times Roman

PRINTED IN U.S.A.

The author assumes full responsibility for the accuracy of all facts and quotations as cited in this book.

Library of Congress Cataloging in Publication Data

Brunt, John, 1943—
    Now & not yet.

    Includes bibliographies.
    1. Eschatology—Biblical teaching.   2. Eschatology.
3. Christian ethics—Seventh-day Adventist authors.
4. Bible. N.T.—Criticism, interpretation, etc.
5. Seventh-day Adventists—Doctrines.   6. Adventists—
Doctrines.   I. Title.
BS2545.E7B78   1987   236   87-4617

ISBN 0-8280-0386-6

*Dedicated to our children
Laura and Larry,
who keep our focus on the future and
fill the present with joy.*

Contents

Preface...11

Chapter One   Daily Business and the Future.............13

Chapter Two   New Testament Eschatology:
    Already—Not Yet.......................................18

Chapter Three   Jesus and the Presence of the
    Kingdom..21

Chapter Four   Jesus and the Nature of the
    Kingdom..25

Chapter Five   The Future Guaranteed: Paul's
    Perspective 29

Chapter Six   Eternal Life Now: John's
    Perspective 36

Chapter Seven   Already, Not Yet, and Now.............42

Chapter Eight   Eschatology and Sexual Ethics...........51

Chapter Nine   Eschatology and Political Ethics..........61

Chapter Ten   Eschatology and Social Ethics 72

Chapter Eleven   The Wedding 83

Preface

In a much-too-kind review of my previous book, *Decisions,** Dr. Gerald Winslow—friend, colleague, and neighbor—suggested that perhaps the cover should have had a different design. The book, which attempts to show how the Bible helps us make ethical decisions, has on the cover a picture of Rodin's *The Thinker*. Winslow suggested that perhaps Da Vinci's *Venus de Milo* might be more appropriate, since he was most intrigued by what was *missing* from the book. For while I presented a general overview of how the Bible aids us in making ethical decisions, I included only a few actual examples of biblical material and its significance for ethics. In this book I shall attempt to begin putting some arms on *Venus* by focusing on one aspect of biblical teaching—eschatology—and surveying how the doctrine of end time contributes to ethics.

The term *eschatology* literally means "a study of last things." I use it in a general way to refer to the cluster of Christian doctrines that has to do with the end of earth's history. This includes the doctrines of the Second Coming, resurrection, and judgment. The term *ethics,* on the other hand, refers to systematic thinking about human moral behavior. Thus we shall attempt to see how Christian thinking about last things contributes to our understanding of the moral life.

I would like to give special thanks to the students in Andrews University's Master of Arts in Religion extension program at Montemorelos University. During the summer of 1981 I had the privilege of teaching a course in eschatology and ethics to this highly motivated, intelligent, and dedicated group of ministers from the Inter-American Division, and this book reflects numerous insights gained during our class discussions.

Endnotes

*John Brunt, *Decisions: How to Use Biblical Guidelines When Making Decisions* (Nashville: Southern Pub. Assn., 1979).

Chapter One

Daily Business and the Future

In his fanciful tale *The Hobbit* J.R.R. Tolkien describes a community of dwarfs who had been displaced from their home by a mean dragon. The dwarfs repeated a legend that one day their former leaders would return and restore their fortunes. They even sang about the coming day when gold would flow in the rivers and when new songs and new laughter would fill the land. However, Tolkien goes on to say, "This pleasant legend did not much affect their daily business."[1]

As Seventh-day Adventists we believe that we have been displaced from our original home. We look forward to a day that is much more than legend, a day that is a firm promise. We too sing and talk of that day when the land will be filled with a new song. But does this hope much affect our daily business? What is the relationship between the future hope and the nitty-gritty of daily life? How does our eschatology make a difference in the way we live now?

The fact is that ideas do have practical consequences in actual life, and theological ideas are no exception. Our ideas about eschatology do more than satisfy our curiosity about the future. They inevitably affect our values and concerns here and now in this world.

Some scholars have suggested that a future-oriented eschatology such as Adventists hold (one that looks forward to an end of this world and the beginning of a new heaven and earth) definitely makes a difference, but only a negative difference. They say that anyone who focuses on the future is likely to ignore responsibility in the present. Only those who have settled down in the world to stay can show the real concern that is needed to make this world a better place.

For instance, Walter Rauschenbusch, the great proponent of the social gospel in early twentieth-century America, argued that the kingdom of God was not a matter of getting individuals to heaven, but of transforming life on earth into the harmony of heaven.[2] He claimed that some Christian bodies are deadweight in this effort at moral reformation because they make central the apocalyptic ideas of early Christianity. Thus they become pessimistic about this world. They can think only about a world to come and thus shirk the responsibility to make this world into God's kingdom.[3]

In a statement that is both more recent and more strident, Jack T. Sanders, a professor of New Testament at the University of Oregon, has argued that the kind of future-oriented eschatology presented in the biblical book of Revelation is evil. It is evil, he insists, because it focuses on something God will do in the very near future to change things. It completely ignores what *we* can and should be doing now to change things. He calls this a "retreat from the ethical dimension," [4] and decries the fact that it is seen in Christians today. He even goes so far as to say:

It is unfortunate that we are today experiencing a revival of just the kind of Christianity found in Revelation; but this revival has its ironically fortunate side in that it permits one to see with all clarity the degree to which such a position is ethically destitute. When persons today consciously and deliberately reject all obligation to help to seek to overcome the social, international, and individual problems of our time and insist that such problems are not the concern of the individual because Jesus is coming soon, we have the ultimate retreat from ethical responsibility. To the degree that the Apocalypse itself contributes to such views today, its existence and its place in the canon are, in the fullest sense of the word, evil.[5]

Certainly it is possible for people to use the Second Coming as an excuse to shun ethical responsibility. But when eschatology is properly understood, exactly the opposite should be true. Eschatology, rather than causing a retreat from ethics, should enhance and motivate ethical responsibility. Eschatology and ethics should go hand in hand.

Unfortunately, Adventists (at least in published literature)[6] have not given much thought to the relationship between eschatology and ethics. In fact, when we think of the Second Coming in relationship to moral responsibility and specific behavior, our thinking turns inevitably to the matter of motivation. In other words, we emphasize eschatology in order to say "Jesus is coming soon, so you'd better be good!" Thus eschatology becomes the scare factor that is supposed to motivate the right kind of ethical behavior.

But this is much too shallow a view of the relationship between eschatology and ethics. In fact, it displays a failure to understand the richness of what the New Testament says about both eschatology and ethics.

First, it fails to understand ethics, because the New Testament consistently offers quite a different motivation and foundation for ethics. The New Testament message is not "Live a life of moral responsibility so that you can go to heaven," but rather "Live a life of moral responsibility because God, by the grace revealed in Jesus Christ, has saved you. Therefore, a moral life is the only appropriate way to respond to His grace.''

Second, it fails to understand eschatology, because it sees only one dimension in eschatology when the New Testament emphasizes two. New Testament teaching about eschatology has not only a future or ''not yet'' dimension but also a past or ''already'' dimension. This latter dimension is especially important in understanding the relationship between eschatology and ethics.

When we understand the true nature of the New Testament's teaching about eschatology, the doctrine of last things becomes more than a sanction that tells the Christian, ''You'd better be good, or else.'' The eschatological vision of our future hope actually contributes to the *content* or shape of our daily lives. It helps us see how we should live responsibly here and now.

But this moves us ahead of the story. Before we continue along this line, we need to come to a clearer understanding of these ''already'' and ''not yet'' aspects of New Testament eschatology. The following chapters will help us do this by surveying the various New Testament writers and their teaching about eschatology.

Endnotes

[1] J.R.R. Tolkien, *The Hobbit: Or There and Back Again* (New York: Ballantine Books, 1966), p. 186.

[2] Walter Rauschenbusch, *Christianity and the Social Crisis* (New York: Macmillan, 1908), p. 65.

[3] *Ibid.*, p. 203.

[4] Jack T. Sanders, *Ethics in the New Testament: Change and Development* (Philadelphia: Fortress, 1975), pp. 113, 114.

[5] *Ibid.*, p. 115.

[6] For two notable exceptions to this general trend see Sakae Kubo, *God Meets Man: A Theology of the Sabbath and the Second Advent* (Nashville: Southern Pub. Assn., 1978), pp. 105-111, and the essays in *Pilgrimage of Hope,* ed. Roy Branson (Takoma Park, Md.: Association of Adventist Forums, 1986).

Chapter Two

New Testament Eschatology: Already—Not Yet

You cannot be an Adventist for very long without seeing last-day events charts. The charts begin with either the Lisbon earthquake in 1755, the end of papal supremacy in 1798, or the great disappointment of 1844. They continue through all the great prophetic events, in chronological order, and end with the Second Coming. The degree of detail often is amazing. Every event, from the little time of trouble to Jacob's time of trouble, from the loud cry to the shaking time, from the early rain to the latter rain, from the close of probation to the seven last plagues, is included.

These charts are not without problems, however. I have yet to see two that are precisely the same. The more detailed they get, the more the disagreements appear. But even beyond this, virtually all share another more serious problem. The list of "last-day" events begins too late. Centuries too late.

The New Testament writers paint the events that already had occurred in the life, death, and resurrection of Jesus as *eschatological.* They applied to what God had accomplished in Jesus Christ at His first coming the very terms, imagery, and motifs that Judaism had reserved for the end of the age. In fact, the New Testament authors claimed that their time was already the last, or final, time. In Acts 2:17 Peter interprets the events of Pentecost as the fulfillment of

Joel's prophecy about the last days. Notice also the following passages from Hebrews and 1 John.

"In the past God spoke to our forefathers through the prophets at many times and in various ways, but in these last days he has spoken to us by his Son, whom he appointed heir of all things, and through whom he made the universe" (Heb. 1:1, 2).

"Dear children, this is the last hour; and as you have heard that the antichrist is coming, even now many antichrists have come. This is how we know it is the last hour" (1 John 2:18).

All these passages use the Greek adjective *eschatos,* from which we get our word *eschatology,* to describe the time of the apostles. For the apostles the resurrection of Christ was *already* an eschatological event. In fact, they believed that it had ushered in the last days. Only language that had previously been reserved for the end of the world could adequately describe the significance of the Resurrection.

Admittedly, all this confuses us somewhat. We tend to bind the term *eschatology* completely to the future. So it is difficult for us to think of past events as eschatology—as difficult as trying to think of square triangles. But this is how the New Testament writers emphasized the decisiveness of Christ's resurrection.

Yet while the authors of the New Testament speak of the past in eschatological terms, they do not deny the significance of future eschatology. In fact, what Christ has already done provides the assurance that His promise about the future is reliable. The *already* provides assurance for the *not yet.*

Now this may sound pretty abstract. We need to make it more concrete by actually looking at the various New Testament writings to see what they teach about eschatology. We particularly need to clarify what they say about the two dimensions, "already" and "not yet." The following brief survey will show that although the terminology the writers used varies considerably, the basic picture remains consistent throughout the New Testament. The next two chapters will focus on Jesus' attitude toward eschatology as seen especially in the Synoptic Gospels, where He so often speaks of the *kingdom*. Then we will turn to the writings of Paul and John.

Chapter Three

Jesus and the Presence of the Kingdom

We most clearly see Jesus' concept of eschatology in His use of the expression "kingdom of God" or "kingdom of heaven." [1] The Jewish world of His day was looking for a kingdom, although few could agree on the precise nature of that kingdom. Some saw it in this-worldly, political terms. Others looked for an other-worldly kingdom that God would usher in after a catastrophic end to this world. For some Jews the Messiah played a prominent role in bringing the kingdom. Others hardly mentioned a Messiah in their eschatological expectations, and still others expected the arrival of two Messiahs. All in all, a variety of beliefs about the future kingdom marked Jewish eschatological thought in Jesus' day.

Jesus startled all these various groups by announcing that the kingdom had already come in His ministry. His ability to cast out demons was the evidence that the kingdom had arrived. Notice Matthew 12:28: "But if I drive out demons by the Spirit of God, then the kingdom of God has come upon you."

Yet Jesus' announcement that the kingdom had already come in no way negates talk about a yet future arrival of the kingdom. In His discourse on the end of the world, recorded in Matthew 24, Mark 13, and Luke 21, Jesus clearly showed that the kingdom appears to be *present yet future at the same time*.

Traditional Adventist theological terminology has recognized this by using the phrases "kingdom of grace" and "kingdom of glory." Kingdom of grace refers to the present aspect of the kingdom, which is available now wherever hearts are open to receive it. Kingdom of glory, on the other hand, refers to the future aspect of the kingdom, which will appear at the second coming of Christ. The terminology is not biblical, but it is helpful as long as we do not misunderstand it. It does not refer to two separate kingdoms that are somehow two different things. There is ultimately only *one* kingdom. The kingdom is where God reigns. It is His rule, or government.

In Jesus Christ, God's rule, usurped by Satan, returns to this world. The Resurrection demonstrated the superiority of God's kingdom and secured God's victorious reign. But this rule is still not fully recognized. Only where it is recognized and accepted does the kingdom of grace prevail. Jesus points forward to a time when the enemy will be completely destroyed and God's kingdom will fill all in all. This is the kingdom of glory. So we have one kingdom and two ways that the kingdom is manifest in two different eras.

This picture of God's reign comes through clearly in Jesus' parables about the kingdom. Conservative theologian George Ladd[2] has shown what these parables contribute to an understanding of the kingdom. They show that the kingdom has already come in the ministry of Jesus but that the end is not yet. In fact, Ladd believes that this fact is the mystery of the kingdom. Most Jews thought that their liberation (which was understood differently by different Jewish groups) would come simultaneously with the kingdom, but Jesus shows that the kingdom arrives in advance of its final manifestation. In the parables Jesus makes known this mystery to the spiritually perceptive.

For example, the parable of the sower shows that in the present the kingdom has only partial success because it is dependent upon the receptiveness of those who hear it. The parable of the tares shows that the kingdom has come without separating the good from the evil in the world. Both righteous and wicked remain in the world. But a final harvest will come when good and evil will be separated and the kingdom will be fully manifest. The parable of the mustard seed shows that while the kingdom appears small and insignificant now, it will eventually fill the world. The parables of the treasures and pearl show the ultimate worth of the kingdom.

Ladd thus sums up the main points that the parables teach about the kingdom. The kingdom is already present in the world with the ministry of Jesus. It appears small and insignificant now, because God's rulership is not recognized by most people, and God allows evil to exist. However, the kingdom will one day fully rule the world. This consummation of the kingdom will be God's act and will come with an apocalyptic harvest, not by gradual growth. Finally, the kingdom is of infinite value. Nothing is more important to any human being.

Thus we see in Jesus' teaching about the kingdom both an already and a not yet. The kingdom of heaven, the focus of eschatology, is already here. The kingdom's decisive victory over evil has already been won. And yet even more has been promised—the final, universal manifestation of the kingdom.[3]

All this means that Christians today live in a unique time. We live during the time between the decisive victory and the end of the war, to use the analogy that theologian Oscar Cullmann made popular.[4] Or to use another analogy, our age is like the end of a lopsided football game. Suppose that with three minutes left in the game the score is 84 to 0. Everyone knows who will win. For all practical purposes, the game is over. Yet the play still goes on. Passes are thrown, tackles are made, and players—even players on the winning side—can still suffer injuries. Yet the outcome of the game itself is sure.

The outcome of our planet's history is certain. The decisive victory is already in the past. The kingdom of heaven has come. And yet we still look forward to its final manifestation. This fact has ethical significance, as we shall see later. But first we need to understand something about the *nature* of this kingdom that broke into our world through Jesus. What does the kingdom stand for? What is it all about?

Endnotes

[1] The scriptural expressions "kingdom of God" and "kingdom of heaven" are synonymous. Mark prefers the former, while Matthew consistently uses the latter. Matthew is probably influenced here by the Jewish practice of using the term *heaven* as a circumlocution for God.

[2] George E. Ladd, *Jesus and the Kingdom: The Eschatology of Biblical Realism* (Waco: Word Books, 1964), pp. 214-238.

[3] For an excellent discussion of the "already" and the "not yet" as it relates to Matthew's Gospel, see William G. Johnsson, *Religion in Overalls* (Nashville: Southern Pub. Assn., 1977), pp. 81-94.

[4] See Oscar Cullmann, *Christ and Time: The Primitive Christian Conception of Time and History,* trans. Floyd V. Filson, rev. ed. (Philadelphia: Westminster, 1964).

Chapter Four

Jesus and the Nature of the Kingdom

Kingdoms—or governments, as we would call them today—usually stand for something. Communities of people are held together only with some kind of ideology. These ideologies can be as different as daylight and darkness, but it takes some kind of vision and symbolic center to weld any group of individuals into a nation. Some nations share a vision of democracy and freedom, some of socio-economic equality, and some of anti-imperialism. Each of these visions results in different values. For example, nations such as the United States value individual freedom above all else, while other governments place little value on it.

The kingdom of heaven, or God's government, as we might say, also stands for something. Jesus' message is not just that the kingdom is already present in the world, or that it will one day fill all in all. He also shows what the kingdom stands for—its nature and its values.

Perhaps the most significant "manifesto" of God's government is Jesus' Sermon on the Mount, in Matthew 5. John R. W. Stott is correct when he labels this sermon a call to a Christian "counterculture."* In it Jesus shows us that God's government is based on values and principles that are not only different from but antithetical to the values of this world's governments. Let's take a look at some of these values as set forth in Jesus' teachings within the book of Matthew, and especially the Sermon on the Mount.

Grace—Jesus tells a strange story in Matthew 20 and likens it to God's government. A landowner hires workers for his vineyard. Some begin work early in the morning. Throughout the day others are added, until finally some join the work crew just one hour before quitting time. Only those hired early in the morning know what their wages will be. The rest hear only that the landowner will pay them what is fair. At the end of the day all receive the very same wage.

We hardly find it surprising that those who worked all day complained. We can't help identifying with them. If we had worked outside in the heat all day, we would expect to get more than those who worked only an hour. It only seems fair. And the fact is, it would *be* fair.

But God's government isn't based on the kind of fairness that rewards people for their achievements. If it were, we would all be in deep trouble. His government is based on grace. The landowner tells the grumbling workers that they shouldn't begrudge his *generosity*. In God's government we are all treated better than we deserve, infinitely better. This undeserved generosity, which God so freely bestows, forms the very foundation of His government.

Humility—In the Beatitudes Jesus shows the characteristics of the true citizen of God's government. Each Beatitude has two parts. In the first part Jesus points to a certain quality, while in the second He promises that these people will be citizens of God's kingdom. It doesn't take long to notice that the qualities Jesus espouses as the characteristics of the citizens of God's government are hardly the qualities valued by this world. The composite picture shows a person who recognizes his or her need for God, who sorrows for sin, and who leads a life of gentleness and peace, even to the point of being willing to suffer persecution.

I saw a cartoon recently that pointed up the difference between this way of life and the values of our world. A man standing on the edge of the world looks up to God and says, "Er, in case You haven't noticed, the meek are getting creamed down here." Our world may value assertiveness and being number one, but God's government values gentleness and humility. It is based on love, not force. Citizens of God's kingdom turn the other cheek, rather than retaliate.

Service—Jesus told His disciples, "You know that those who are regarded as rulers of the Gentiles lord it over them, and their high officials exercise authority over them. Not so with you. Instead, whoever wants to become great among you must be your servant, and whoever wants to be first must be slave of all. For even the Son of Man did not come to be served, but to serve, and to give his life as a ransom for many" (Mark 10:42-45).

God's government values service over status and success. Just as Jesus came to serve, so the person who responds to God's grace, revealed in Jesus, will value life as an opportunity for service.

Just this brief survey of some of the values of God's government reveals the difference between His government and the governments that we know in this world. Worldly governments have to devote their energies to defense and military force in order to survive. But Jesus boldly declares that these appearances are deceiving. In the long run, it is love, not force; service, not status; humility, not hubris; that will have the last word. God's government offers an alternative counterculture to this world, and in the end all will see that what it values is the same as that which endures for eternity.

But Jesus does more than proclaim that God's government will win in the end. He invites us to enter it now. His most surprising announcement is that we can live as citizens of God's government now.

We know that there are places in the world where more than one government can occupy the same geographical territory. Within the same village some may be loyal to an existing dictator and others to a revolutionary force seeking to overthrow the dictator. Naturally, such cases produce conflict and often violence.

According to Jesus, we can begin now, within the context of our sinful world, to respond to His message of grace. Our lives can show our loyalty to the values of God's government. Jesus does far more than tell us to be good so that in the future we can enter heaven. Rather He invites us to join a revolutionary government whose values are different, and to begin living by those values now. He assures us that when we become citizens of this new government we are joining up with a government that will not only win in the end, but will endure forever.

We shall talk more about the ethical significance of the nature of God's kingdom later, but now we turn to other New Testament writings to survey their perspective on eschatology.

Endnotes

*John R. W. Stott, *The Message of the Sermon on the Mount* (Downers Grove, Ill.: Inter-Varsity Press, 1978).

Chapter Five

The Future Guaranteed: Paul's Perspective

One year I taught a class on Paul's letters that met the first period in the morning. In those days school started earlier than it does now, and in the middle of winter first period began before the sun came up. One especially cold, dark midwinter morning, with snow on the ground and stars twinkling in the sky, I greeted a class of freshman students. Most of them were only half awake, and I'm sure some of them had managed to pull themselves out of bed no more than five minutes earlier. I opened class by asking, "How many of you feel that you have already gone to heaven and are now at the right hand of God's throne?"

I have never had people look at me as though I were quite so crazy!

After all, it does sound preposterous. We have only to look around to see that our environment is a far cry from heaven. And if looking around doesn't do it, certainly a glance at the morning paper will. And most apparent of all are the weaknesses that mark our lives—if we will take that painful look.

Yet incredible as it may seem, Paul in Ephesians 1 and 2 presents Christian hope in precisely those terms. In chapter 1, verse 18 he speaks of the *hope* to which God has called us. He then goes on to speak of the great power and might that God "exerted in Christ when he raised him from the dead and seated him at his right hand in the heavenly realms, far above all rule and authority, power and dominion, and every title that can be given, not only in the present age but also in the one to come. And God placed all things under his feet and appointed him to be head over everything for the church'' (verses 20-22).

Now, the fact that Jesus has been raised and exalted to the right hand of God is easy enough for us to believe. Those terms do not strain our credulity. But Paul doesn't stop here. He goes on to speak of the results of Christ's resurrection and exaltation for us. (Notice especially the emphasized sections in the following passage.)

''As for you, you were dead in your transgressions and sins, in which you used to live when you followed the ways of this world and of the ruler of the kingdom of the air, the spirit who is now at work in those who are disobedient. All of us also lived among them at one time, gratifying the cravings of our sinful nature and following its desires and thoughts. Like the rest, we were by nature objects of wrath. But because of his great love for us, *God,* who is rich in mercy, *made us alive with Christ* even when we were dead in transgressions—it is by grace you have been saved. And God *raised us up with Christ and seated us with him in the heavenly realms* in Christ Jesus, in order that in the coming ages he might show the incomparable riches of his grace, expressed in his kindness to us in Christ Jesus'' (Eph. 2:1-7).

Paul proclaims that we too have been raised and sit in heavenly places with Christ. Given what our senses tell us about our present environment, what can he possibly mean?

Obviously Paul is not speaking literally here. On the other hand, it would certainly be a mistake to brush aside this language as merely symbolic. We must give adequate attention to the radical message Paul is communicating with

30

these words. Paul is saying that Christ's victory is so certain and decisive that it is *already* our victory if we are in Christ. Paul could not say this if our resurrection and exaltation were in any way based on our own goodness or works. Were that the case, our own experience would prove him false. But Paul makes it clear that this salvation, about which he speaks in such radical and almost unbelievable terms, is based solely on God's grace.

"For it is by grace you have been saved, through faith— and this not from yourselves, it is the gift of God—not by works, so that no one can boast" (Eph. 2:8, 9).

When we accept God's grace offered in Christ, Christ's victory is our victory. Already we have passed from death to life. This change is so radical that Paul can speak about it in eschatological terms. We already sit with Christ in heavenly places. And yet this beautiful, symbolic portrayal of the reality of our present life in Christ in no way denies the literal, future Second Coming. Notice how Paul speaks of the "coming ages" in Ephesians 2:7. In fact, Paul's belief in the future aspect of eschatology is seen continuously throughout his letters. In addition to his more detailed treatment of the Second Coming in passages like 1 Thessalonians 4, 2 Thessalonians 2, and 1 Corinthians 15, he constantly uses phrases like "the end" and the "day" of our Lord Jesus.

Rather than ruling out future eschatology, this "already" aspect of eschatology provides the assurance for the future. A word that Paul uses in Ephesians 1:14 vividly points this out. He says that the Holy Spirit, given to us in the present, is our "guarantee" of our future inheritance until we acquire possession of it.

Unfortunately, the English word *guarantee* doesn't communicate the full significance of the word Paul uses. Paul's word refers to the down payment, or earnest money, that one pays to assure that he or she is going to go ahead with the transaction and eventually pay the remainder of the amount of sale. Paul is saying that we have already received the down payment of our salvation, and that down payment assures us that the remaining balance (the ''not yet'' aspect of eschatology) will be ours as well. Again in Paul the present and the promised future come together.

We find a final evidence of this in Paul's use of the concept of the two ages, the present age and the age to come. For Paul, the difference between the two is not just chronological, it is moral. The two ages are shaped by different values. The pattern, or shape, of this present world is characterized by evil. Jesus Christ reveals a different pattern, which will characterize the world to come.

As we would expect in the light of what we have already seen, however, for Paul the world to come is not just something in the future. We can already begin a way of life that fits its pattern, or shape. Paul makes this clear in Romans 12:1, 2: ''Therefore, I urge you, brothers, in view of God's mercy, to offer your bodies as living sacrifices, holy and pleasing to God—which is your spiritual worship. Do not conform any longer to the pattern of this world, but be transformed by the renewing of your mind. Then you will be able to test and approve what God's will is—his good, pleasing and perfect will.''

In 1 Corinthians 7 Paul is even more explicit. He says, ''What I mean, brothers, is that the time is short. From now on those who have wives should live as if they had none; those who mourn, as if they did not; those who are happy, as if they were not; those who buy something, as if it were not theirs to keep; those who use the things of the world, as if not engrossed in them. For this world in its present form is passing away'' (verses 29-31).

Paul is not advocating escape from the world. His words

could be easily misunderstood. In these words he disparages neither sexual relations in marriage (as we will clearly see in chapter eight) nor normal commerce and activity. But he is advocating a stance toward this world that recognizes it for what it is, a temporary home whose rulers reign only as ''lame ducks.'' We must not be ultimately shaped by this world's pattern but by the morally superior pattern of love that characterized Jesus' life and will characterize the world to come.

Paul calls us to let the future begin now. The not yet has everything to do with the now.

Appendix to Chapter Five

A clear understanding of the ''already'' aspect of New Testament eschatology is helpful for understanding a topic that has recently been problematic in Adventism. The message of the book of Hebrews regarding the sanctuary in heaven is similar to the symbolic portrayal of the ''already'' in passages such as Ephesians 2.

In Hebrews 4-10 the sanctuary of Old Testament times is contrasted with the salvation Christ brings. The Most Holy Place of that sanctuary is seen as *the* symbol par excellence of God's presence.

In Old Testament times a barrier stood between that presence of God and the people. The people could not even get near the Most Holy Place. Not even the priests could enter. Only the high priest could go in, and then only once a year. Even then they entered with fear and trembling.

Hebrews contrasts this with the results of Jesus' victory. Jesus opens the way to the presence of God so that *all* may have *continuous, confident* access to God. He by virtue of His death and resurrection (Heb. 9:26) has entered the very presence of God, symbolized by the Most Holy Place (Heb. 6:19; 8:1; 9:12). But that is not all. This is not just a message about heavenly geography. The real point in Hebrews is not simply where Christ is, but what He has done for us. He has opened the way so that we now may be in the Most Holy Place as well. We go through the curtain with Jesus, as we read in Hebrews 10:19-22, a passage that serves as the conclusion of the discussion about the sanctuary: "Therefore, brothers, since we have confidence to enter the Most Holy Place by the blood of Jesus, by a new and living way opened for us through the curtain, that is, his body, and since we have a great priest over the house of God, let us draw near to God with a sincere heart in full assurance of faith, having our hearts sprinkled to cleanse us from a guilty conscience and having our bodies washed with pure water."

In other words, we can *now* confidently enter the presence of God. In Christ, the old barriers that stood between us and God are shattered. This beautiful message of continuous, confident access to God, and the assurance it brings us, is not only where the discussion of the sanctuary in Hebrews ends; it is where it begins. Notice how this introductory statement at the beginning of the discussion of the sanctuary in Hebrews fits in with the conclusion quoted above. It serves to bracket the entire topic.

"Therefore, since we have a great high priest who has gone through the heavens, Jesus the Son of God, let us hold firmly to the faith we profess. For we do not have a high priest who is unable to sympathize with our weaknesses, but we have one who has been tempted in every way, just as we are—yet was without sin. Let us then approach the throne of grace with confidence, so that we may receive mercy and find grace to help us in our time of need" (Heb. 4:14-16).

It is a mistake to use Hebrews to try to solve questions

about the chronology and geography of Christ's ministry in heaven. Hebrews presents a symbolic portrayal of our access to God through Christ. Its message that Christ has opened the way for us now to be in the Most Holy Place of the heavenly sanctuary can no more be taken literally than can Paul's message that we have already been exalted to the "heavenly realms" at the right hand of God in Ephesians 2:6.

But both messages point to a present experience that is very real. Already we realize the results of Christ's victory in our lives by having access to God.

Chapter Six

Eternal Life Now: John's Perspective

We now turn to the writings of John, first the Gospel, then the book of Revelation.

Some scholars have claimed that John no longer believed in a literal return of Christ in the future. They insist that John made all eschatology a matter of the "already." They can only hold this position, however, by concluding that certain verses in John were later additions and do not reflect John's theology. There is no evidence from the ancient manuscripts of John to support these conclusions, which are thus unwarranted and unnecessary. When we take all that John says, we again have a strong emphasis on both the "already" and the "not yet" of eschatology. John's *terminology,* however, differs from both the Synoptic Gospels and Paul.

In John, the key term is *life* or *eternal life*. We often think of eternal life as synonymous with the Christian's future reward. But this is not true for John. He (through the words of Jesus) speaks of eternal life in the present tense. Eternal life is a present reality for Christians. Notice John 5:24: "I tell you the truth, whoever hears my word and believes him who sent me has eternal life and will not be condemned; he has crossed over from death to life."

One who believes in Christ already has eternal life. This gift of life gives assurance. The believer no longer has to fear judgment. The message is as radical as that which we saw in Paul, even though the language differs. In fact, the message is really the same. Paul says that in Christ we are already exalted to the heavenly places with Christ, while John says that when we believe in Christ we already have eternal life.

Again, however, John in no way intends to deny the future aspect of eschatology. In fact, in the verses that follow John 5:24 he ties the two aspects together beautifully. John compares and contrasts the resurrection that now is with that which is coming.

First he says: "I tell you the truth, a time is coming and has now come when the dead will hear the voice of the Son of God and those who hear will live. For as the Father has life in himself, so he has granted the Son to have life in himself. And he has given him authority to judge because he is the Son of Man" (verses 25-27).

Notice that in these verses Jesus is talking about something that now is. Obviously He is referring not to the final resurrection but to the present new life that the believer finds in Him. But this is not the whole story. John goes on to record the following words of Jesus:

"Do not be amazed at this, for a time *is coming* when all who are in their graves will hear his voice and come out—those who have done good will rise to live, and those who have done evil will rise to be condemned" (John 5:28, 29).

John (through the words of Jesus) is talking about an hour that is coming. It is still future. There will be a resurrection when the dead literally come forth. The "already" and the "not yet" are again linked together. This kind of relationship between the "already" and the "not yet" is typical of John. Believers have eternal life now, and in addition, Christ will raise them at the last day.

37

Notice the following verse: "Jesus said to them, 'I tell you the truth, unless you eat the flesh of the Son of Man and drink his blood, you have no life in you. Whoever eats my flesh and drinks my blood has eternal life, and I will raise him up at the last day' '' (John 6:53, 54).

In some ways the Epistles of John and the book of Revelation carry this idea even further. In a later chapter we will examine in more detail certain passages from these works, but at this point we shall consider only one aspect of the message of the book of Revelation.

Revelation

We often miss much of what this book might say to us because we see it only as a book that portrays past and future events through the use of strange, exotic symbols. We fail to recognize two important facts. First, this book communicated a spiritual message of comfort and encouragement to its original readers. It offered believers in the troubled work of first-century Asia Minor a message of hope that holds significance for us as well. Second and closely related, the symbols of Revelation that point to the future hope also have significance for the present experience of the Christian. Revelation links the promised future with the present.

For example, Revelation 2:7 promises the believers in Ephesus that those who conquer will "eat from the tree of life, which is in the paradise of God." This is a future promise. And yet Ellen White, with great insight into the way Revelation uses symbols, says: "Must we wait until we are translated before we eat of the leaves of the tree of life? He who receives into his heart the words of Christ knows what it means to eat the leaves of the tree of life. [John

6:33-63 quoted.] When the believer, in the fellowship of the Spirit, can lay his hand upon truth itself, and appropriate it, he eats the bread that comes down from heaven. He enters into the life of Christ, and appreciates the great sacrifice made in behalf of the sinful race.''*

The promised future can already be realized in an anticipatory way in the present.

The promised ''new song'' offers another example. We first hear of a new song in Revelation 5. When the Lamb, the only one worthy to open the scroll, steps forward to take it, the twenty-four elders and the four living creatures join in singing a new song: ''You are worthy to take the scroll and to open its seals, because you were slain, and with your blood you purchased men for God from every tribe and language and people and nation. You have made them to be a kingdom and priests to serve our God, and they will reign on the earth'' (verses 9, 10).

When the song is concluded, John goes on to tell us: ''Then I looked and heard the voice of many angels, numbering thousands upon thousands, and ten thousand times ten thousand. They encircled the throne and the living creatures and the elders. In a loud voice they sang: 'Worthy is the Lamb, who was slain, to receive power and wealth and wisdom and strength and honor and glory and praise!' Then I heard every creature in heaven and on earth and under the earth and on the sea, and all that is in them, singing: 'To him who sits on the throne and to the Lamb be praise and honor and glory and power, for ever and ever.' The four living creatures said, 'Amen,' and the elders fell down and worshiped'' (verses 11-14).

We hear of the new song again in Revelation 14:1-3, when John tells us about the 144,000. ''Then I looked, and there before me was the Lamb, standing on Mount Zion, and with him 144,000 who had his name and his Father's name written on their foreheads. And I heard a sound from heaven like the roar of rushing waters and like a loud peal of thunder. The sound I heard was like that of harpists playing their harps. And they sang a new song before the throne and before the four living creatures and the elders. No one could learn the song except the 144,000 who had been redeemed from the earth'' (Rev. 14:1-3).

Not only do those who guard God's throne sing a new song about the salvation the Lamb provides; God's people have the privilege of singing it too. But again this promise is linked subtly to the present. Early church historians point out that these great hymns, sung by angels in Revelation, are closely related to, if not based upon, the hymnody of early Christianity. John apparently took the hymnological practice of the early church and placed it in a celestial context. The resulting idea is that Christians, when they sing hymns in their worship services, are already anticipating the promise of singing a new song in God's future kingdom.

I imagine that with all the threat of persecution Christians in a city like Thyatira or Pergamum were facing, the act of gathering in a little house church to worship and sing hymns must have seemed rather insignificant to some. But here John lifts the veil (the title of this book means "unveiling," and it is an unveiling of not only the future but also of the true significance of the present) and lets those worshipers see that they are not just a little, insignificant, persecuted minority in the vast Roman Empire. He lets them see that through the worship and fellowship of the church they are participating with the angels of heaven and anticipating the day when Christ's victory will be fully manifest. Again not yet and now meet. (If we really heard and believed this message, I wonder what it would do for the enthusiasm of our participation in congregational singing!)

Thus even Revelation, the book that seems so oriented to the future, demonstrates the dual character of New Testament eschatology by including both the "already" as well as the "not yet."

Endnotes

* *The SDA Bible Commentary,* Ellen G. White Comments, vol. 7, p. 957.

Chapter Seven

Already, Not Yet, and Now

We have completed our brief survey of the New Testament. Let's summarize what we have found. Then we will ask what difference it all makes.

The picture throughout the New Testament is clear. What God has done for us in Christ and the new experience we enjoy with Him as a result are of such a decisive character that the New Testament writers could speak of them already in eschatological terms. Indeed, these terms and images previously reserved for the end of the world are the only ones adequate to describe Christ's victory and our new experience that results from His grace. But as pointed out before, this "already" of eschatology in no way detracts from the "not yet." Rather than replacing the promise of Christ's literal return, it undergirds it by giving it shape and surety. Because of the "already," we can confidently look forward to the fulfillment of the promise.

Probably for most of us the greatest defect in our eschatology has been our failure to appropriate the assurance of the "already" into our experience. Granted, it is often difficult to make sense out of metaphors that compare our present lives with the resurrection or that speak of us as being already exalted to heavenly places. Our problem is that we don't *feel* that way. We must recognize, however, that this message far transcends our feelings. As finite humans we are subject to emotional ups and downs. But feelings are by no means a trustworthy indication of our spiritual condition. In fact, as my wife and I once discovered, they do not even reliably indicate our physical condition.

Ione had had the flu for several days and felt unusually ill. Since this was very unusual for her, I began to worry. The next day she was even worse, and then I really worried. I decided that she must see a physician. Ione objected because she didn't feel well enough to get out of bed and go to the office, but finally she gave in.

Several weeks earlier I had been sick, although by this time I felt fine. A little cough had hung on, but it didn't bother me at all. As the physician examined her, however, he heard my cough and thought he should also take an X-ray of my chest.

After some waiting the physician sat us both down and said he wanted to talk with us. Ione was still so sick she could hardly sit up, but he told her that she had a viral flu bug. It couldn't really be treated, but it would go away in a few days. He said, "I'm not worried at all about you."

Then he turned to me. I still felt great, but he told me, "I *am* worried about you. I want you home in bed. You've got pneumonia, and unless you promise to take care of yourself you're going to the hospital." Then he turned back to Ione and said, "I want you to make sure he stays in bed. Don't even let him get up to eat. You take his meals and medicine to him in bed and make sure he stays there." Needless to say, that wasn't very good news for her!

Just as our feelings were rather poor indicators of our real physical condition, so we must not base our spiritual experience on mere feelings. The exalted picture of new life in Christ that the New Testament portrays is based not on our feelings but upon God's Word, and we can trust His Word. If we will trust God, not only are the promises ours, but also the present is already an anticipation of and partial realization of those promises. And it is all thanks to Christ's victory and to God's generosity in offering us the benefits of that victory. And once this happens in our lives, it makes a difference—a difference that is especially significant for ethics.

This New Testament message of eschatology, with its "already" and its "not yet" aspects, impinges on ethics in at least two major ways. First, it relates to the motivation for and the general character of the moral life. Second, the uniquely Christian vision of the future helps give specific shape to the moral life.

At one time or another we have all heard sermons on the Second Coming that were designed to put the "fear of the Lord" in us. We saw vividly portrayed the swift and sure rewards for disobedience that were just around the corner. We probably went home a bit frightened, wondering if there was any chance that we would ever make it. Such sermons definitely have an effect on our lives, and no one can deny that there are biblical warnings about fire and brimstone. But such sermons also hold a certain danger.

I have been amazed how many of us who have been reared Adventists can recall similar childhood dreams. Jesus is coming, and we know that we are not ready. We want to cry out, "This is our God, we have waited for Him," as we know we should. But instead, the rocks and mountains start falling on us.

All this presents the danger that the gospel will become something like the good-news, bad-news jokes that were popular some time ago. You remember the kind: The good news is that for your birthday I made the down payment on a new Rolls Royce for you. However, the bad news is that it was only five dollars, and you're not going to believe the monthly payments.

Here's the danger. When someone uses eschatology to

put "the fear of the Lord" in us and motivate us to good behavior, the good news of the gospel becomes bad news. The good news is that you have been freely saved by grace. The bad news is that Jesus is coming soon to judge you by your works, and you're probably not good enough to make it. Somehow at this point the doctrines of salvation and eschatology don't seem to fit together properly.

But those two doctrines come together when we realize that the salvation Christ has already provided for us is the eschatological down payment of our future inheritance. There is no separation between salvation and eschatology. The "already" and the "not yet" are but two aspects of the same salvation event. Christ has already opened His kingdom to us and given us eternal life.

This means that we can do nothing to earn our present or future salvation. The life we live is not *so that* He might save us, but *because* He has *already* saved us. It is a response to God's love and generosity, not an effort to convince Him to change His mind about us. Now make no mistake about it, it is possible to reject God's generous gift of salvation. God gives us that freedom. But if we recognize God's generosity and accept His gift, we will naturally want to respond appropriately to Him.

For this reason we see a repeated sequence in Paul's letters. Paul begins in the indicative mode. He tells of what Christ has already done for us. He paints this "already" in eschatological terms that are almost too beautiful and idyllic for us to imagine. He makes it clear that this is by no means our own doing. There is *never* anything about which we can boast. He also makes it clear that this "already" is only the beginning, the down payment which assures that Christ will do even more and grant us the full inheritance.

But after all this, Paul usually says, "Therefore," and moves to the imperative mode. (See Romans 12:1, Galatians 5:1, and Ephesians 4:1 for examples of this transition in his letters.) He is saying, if you appreciate what God has done for you and are grasped by His love, here is the only appropriate way to respond. If you appreciate the inheritance God has provided for you and look forward to the day when it will be fully manifest, then by all means, begin now to live consistently with that inheritance.

For example, after presenting the beautiful message of Ephesians 1 and 2, Paul makes the transition to the second half of the book, which focuses on ethics, by saying: "As a prisoner for the Lord, then, I urge you to live a life worthy of the calling you have received. Be completely humble and gentle; be patient, bearing with one another in love. Make every effort to keep the unity of the Spirit through the bond of peace" (Eph. 4:1-3). In the light of our calling, how could we possibly respond in any other way than by living worthily of that calling?

Both the "already" and the "not yet" aspects of eschatology play a role in motivating this "worthy" life. The Christian life is the appropriate response both to what God has done and to what He has promised to do. But this is different from the kind of eschatological motivation about which we spoke at the beginning of the chapter. The *basic* motivation is not hope for reward, or fear of punishment, but response to a person.

Even on this earth, the actions that we find most worthy of praise and emulation are not actions motivated by reward and punishment, but those that flow from genuine love for others. We joke about the boy scout who helps the elderly woman across the street because he has to do it to earn his merit badge. On the other hand, who is not moved by an act of genuine self-sacrifice?

We need to be clear about the basic motivation for the Christian life. Once we realize that Christians live their lives as a response to God, who freely provides salvation and then promises to do even more by allowing us to live with Him for all eternity, then certain facts about the general character of the Christian life are implied:

First, belief in the soon return of Jesus should never be a deterrent to responsible action here and now. Those whose lives are motivated by appreciation for God's generosity have a new love for all of God's children. They know that each person is one whom God loves and for whom Christ died. Such a person can never be unconcerned about the needs and sufferings of other people merely because it will all be taken care of when Jesus comes. (We will say much more about this in chapter ten.)

Second, the cosmological "already/not yet" has implications for the individual life as well. Just as the kingdom has already come to this world, yet awaits its final manifestation, so the individual life has already been transformed by God's grace, even though final perfection comes only in the future. Thus the New Testament writers can employ strong and descriptive language to affirm the newness of the Christian life: "Therefore, if anyone is in Christ, he is a new creation; the old has gone, the new has come! All this is from God, who reconciled us to himself through Christ and gave us the ministry of reconciliation: that God was reconciling the world to himself in Christ, not counting men's sins against them. And he has committed to us the message of reconciliation" (2 Cor. 5:17-19).

But the same Paul who wrote these beautiful words about the "already" of Christian existence also recognized a "not yet" in his own life. After speaking of his desire to attain the resurrection, he went on to say: "Not that I have already obtained all this, or have already been made perfect, but I press on to take hold of that for which Christ Jesus took hold of me. Brothers, I do not consider myself yet to have taken hold of it. But one thing I do: Forgetting what is behind and straining toward what is ahead, I press on toward the goal to win the prize for which God has called me heavenward in Christ Jesus'' (Phil. 3:12-14).

The present Christian life is not one of absolute, sinless perfection. Christians must live with their own weaknesses. Yet the good news of what God's grace has already done gives hope and assurance that ''he who began a good work in you will bring it to completion at the day of Jesus Christ'' (Phil. 1:6, RSV). This assurance protects Christians from discouragement over the weaknesses that remain. It also keeps them from a false self-confidence that is satisfied and no longer feels a need to grow. Like the world as a whole, the Christian moral life knows an ''already'' and a ''not yet.''

Third, the Christian ethic will not be legalistic. Christians do not obey rules in order to get to heaven. They respond to a generous God by living in ways that show their appreciation and desire to please Him. But this in no way minimizes the significance of law or the specific instruction of Scripture. When one responds positively to God's gift of salvation, the desire to please God is spontaneous. However, the specific information about what actions please God is not spontaneous. Thus in the law God has graciously provided us with information about the principles of His character and kingdom, so that we will know how to respond appropriately to Him.

Jesus makes it clear in the Sermon on the Mount that we must not understand these laws in a merely literalistic way. We do not obey in order to receive a reward. Rather, the law reveals the principles that will motivate those who want to please God and who desire to begin living now according to the principles of the kingdom to which He calls us.

(We might mention on the side that all this has implications for our evangelism as well. Our task is not to use scare tactics to warn of an impending disaster. Rather we proclaim that the kingdom, in partial manifestation, is already here. We can now begin to enjoy its fruits. But even more, we proclaim the additional good news that the day when the Saviour's promise finds its final fulfillment and when the kingdom is fully manifest is near at hand. That is all the more reason to respond to and accept this wonderful gift.)

It is not only the law and specific commands in Scripture that reveal the principles of God's character and kingdom to us, however. The vision of the future that God is preparing for us also reveals His will. God has revealed many specific details about the future not simply to satisfy our curiosity, or even to give us hope, as important as that is. Eschatology tells us what kind of God we serve by revealing what He values and wants to make part of the future world.

I have a simple assignment that I have sometimes used in Weeks of Prayer with kids. I have them write out what one thing they would do to change the world if they had the chance. Their answers tell me a lot about their values. For instance, if a fellow says that he would change the world to make baseball season last all year, it's not hard to figure out what he enjoys and values.

The vision of the new world to come also tells us a lot about God. And this in turn tells us about our responsibility to live according to His will. In other words, the shape of our eschatology has profound implications for the specific shape of our ethics.

This is why biblical writers can use specific facts about the future to motivate our present actions. For example, Paul was concerned about the way members of the church at Corinth were relating to each other. Not only was the church divided into various factions that gave allegiance to different leaders (see 1 Cor. 1:12) but members were taking their fellow members to civil courts in litigation over trivial matters.

In 1 Corinthians 6 Paul addresses this problem by using several arguments. He even reasons that it would be better for them to suffer wrong and be defrauded than to threaten both the unity of the church and its influence in the community. One of Paul's arguments is clearly eschatological: "If any of you has a dispute with another, dare he take it before the ungodly for judgment instead of before the saints? Do you not know that the saints will judge the world? And if you are to judge the world, are you not competent to judge trivial cases? Do you not know that we will judge angels? How much more the things of this life!" (1 Cor. 6:1-3).

Paul appeals to the eschatological vision. One day God will give the saints the privilege of affirming God's judgment. In fact, they will judge the world. They will even judge angels! For Paul that vision is not simply a fact about the future. It should also motivate how we live in the present. Can't people with such a future be responsible and sensible enough to settle trivial cases here and now? If the future vision really lives in their hearts, they ought to lead lives consistent with it. There is a relationship between the not yet and the now.

The next three chapters take up three topics which illustrate that relationship. They discuss what our eschatology teaches about the ethics of sex, response to oppression, and our relationship to society and its needs.

Chapter Eight

Eschatology and Sexual Ethics

Perhaps you wonder what sex and the Second Coming have to do with each other. Did you know that in one of the most important New Testament passages about sexuality, Paul appeals to an aspect of eschatology? He tells us that if we understand the significance of the doctrine of the resurrection, we will see implications for sexuality.

The passage is found in 1 Corinthians 6:12–7:5. Let's read the entire passage first. We will then examine the circumstances surrounding its writing, and finally we'll discuss its significance for the question of eschatology and ethics.

"Everything is permissible for me"—but not everything is beneficial. "Everything is permissible for me"—but I will not be mastered by anything. "Food for the stomach and the stomach for food"—but God will destroy them both. The body is not meant for sexual immorality, but for the Lord, and the Lord for the body. By his power God raised the Lord from the dead, and he will raise us also.

Do you not know that your bodies are members of Christ himself? Shall I then take the members of Christ and unite them with a prostitute? Never! Do you not know that he who unites himself with a prostitute is one with her in body? For it is said, "The two will become one flesh." But he who unites himself with the Lord is one with him in spirit.

Flee from sexual immorality. All other sins a man commits are outside his body, but he who sins sexually sins against his own body. Do you not know that your body is a temple of the Holy Spirit, who is in you, whom you have received from God? You are not your own; you were bought at a price. Therefore honor God with your body.

Now for the matters you wrote about: It is good for a man not to marry. But since there is so much immorality, each man should have his own wife, and each woman her own husband. The husband should fulfill his marital duty to his wife, and likewise the wife to her husband. The wife's body does not belong to her alone but also to her husband. In the same way, the husband's body does not belong to him alone but also to his wife. Do not deprive each other except by mutual consent and for a time, so that you may devote yourselves to prayer. Then come together again so that Satan will not tempt you because of your lack of self-control.

Paul is not simply writing a treatise about sexuality. Rather he is addressing a specific problem in a specific city. In order to understand what Paul is saying, we need to understand something about the situation to which he speaks.

A number of elements in 1 Corinthians indicate that in Corinth at least some people were being influenced by ideas similar to what would become the heresy of Gnosticism in the second century. Several characteristics of this type of thinking show up in 1 Corinthians, but one in particular interests us here. Those with a Gnostic-type perspective emphasized a sharp dichotomy between matter and spirit. They believed that all matter, including the human body, was evil. In their eschatology they looked forward to a time after death when they would be freed from all material existence. No longer would they be imprisoned in a body.

This type of thinking led to two quite different approaches to sexuality.

Some said that since the body is evil anyway, it doesn't really matter what you do with it. After all, it is just a temporary entity soon to be destroyed. Nothing done with or to the body could in any way affect the real person. Therefore they allowed any sexual activity in or out of marriage.

Others, however, concluded that since the body is evil, bodily activities are also evil. They believed that all forms of sexual expression, in or out of marriage, were wrong. If they permitted marriage at all, they demanded that the married couple live together as brother and sister—in celibacy. Apparently Christians had espoused both types of thinking in Corinth.

Biblical scholars have discovered that Paul often quotes what the Corinthians were saying and then responds to them. A general consensus has emerged that when Paul makes a statement followed by "but" and goes on to refute the statement, the statement is one of the Corinthian slogans. Our passage contains several such statements. And they seem to represent both kinds of gnostic thinking with regard to sexuality.

On the one hand, certain Corinthians were saying, "It is well for a man not to touch a woman" (1 Cor. 7:1, RSV). Notice that in the first half of that verse, Paul says he is taking up the questions that the Corinthians had asked in their letter to him. So apparently this was one of the statements they made. Notice also that immediately following the statement, Paul says "but" and goes on to disagree with the idea. Thus it appears that this was a Corinthian slogan expressing the views of those who thought that anything having to do with the body was evil.

On the other hand, other Corinthians seem to have been saying, "All things are lawful for [us]" (1 Cor. 6:12, RSV). Again Paul follows with the word "but" and a refutation.

In a recent article Jerome Murphy-O'Connor[1] has examined the structure of this passage. He concludes that the assertion "Food is meant for the stomach and the stomach for food—and God will destroy both one and the other" (verse 13, RSV) was another Corinthian slogan. In fact, he goes on to argue that the Corinthians also made a parallel statement that Paul does not quote but only refutes. They in effect said, "Sex is meant for the body and the body for sex—and God will destroy both one and the other." Both statements reflect the idea that since the body was evil anyway, no bodily activity could affect spirituality. Therefore, all things were lawful.

Paul addresses both positions in our passage. In 1 Corinthians 6:12-20 he refutes the position that sexual activity is unrelated to spirituality. The Corinthians said that the body is meant for sex, but Paul has a different view of the body. His position is based squarely on his eschatology. Paul believes that when Jesus returns, He will resurrect the body. The apostle believes in a body with a future.[2] Furthermore, that future says something about the present.

According to Murphy-O'Connor (in the article already referred to), Paul actually takes the structure of the Corinthian statement and rewrites it according to his view of the resurrection. They say: "The body is for sex, and sex is for the body. The one and the other God will destroy." But Paul says the body is not for immorality, and counters: "The body is for the Lord, and the Lord is for the body. God raised Jesus and He will raise us." The body's future is not destruction but resurrection. Therefore, the body should be treated consistently with its exalted future.

Paul then goes on to spell out what sexual activities are and are not appropriate to that future. He says that God has put within the sexual relationship the power to help bring about total oneness between a man and a woman. God's purpose is that the two shall become one. But it is inconsistent to take the body, which belongs to the Lord and is destined for resurrection, and make it one with a prostitute. This produces a perverted oneness. It is a sin against one's own body. It is inconsistent with the indwelling of the Holy Spirit in the body.

In other words, for Paul, what one does with the body *is* important. We should glorify God in the body. We should use the body in a way consistent with God's purpose for it. God approves of sexual expression that is a part of the total oneness of a man and woman who make a complete, lifelong commitment to each other. God wants two people to become one in the marriage relationship. He wants the family to be a blessing to individuals and society. He created sexual expression to be enjoyed as a part of and an aid toward the total oneness of two people who have committed their lives to each other.

Thus Paul also says no to those who take the opposite position and forbid all sexual expression. Contrary to their belief, the body and anything having to do with it are *not* evil. The resurrection of the body affirms the goodness of the body when used according to God's purpose. The body is not a prison from which one will eventually find escape. The body can actually be used to glorify God. Thus in 1 Corinthians 7:1-5 Paul refutes the statement that even in marriage a man is not to touch a woman.

Paul says that husband and wife should give to each other their conjugal rights. If they refrain from sexual activity during a period of intensive devotion and prayer, it should be only for a short time and by mutual consent. Their bodies belong to each other.

Paul expresses here a picture of the mutuality of the marriage relationship that is unusual for his day. Paul is often accused of being a male chauvinist. When we consider his writings carefully, however, this is certainly not the case. In verse 4 Paul says that the wife does not rule over her own body, but the husband does. Such a statement would not have been at all unusual in Paul's day. But what Paul goes on to say would have been very unusual. He says that in the same way the husband does not rule over his own body, but the wife does. Paul sees the relationship as one of mutuality. Sexual expression is based on a mutuality. Both marital partners belong to each other. Paul affirms genuine oneness.

Therefore, Paul clearly maintains a connection between sex and the Second Coming. The recognition that the body will be resurrected at the Second Coming and that the Christian hope includes a place for the body has implications for understanding sexuality. If one's view of last-day events sees the future as a time of escape from an evil body, it is only logical that the body should now be viewed as either evil or insignificant. As a result, sexual expression is either prohibited altogether or approved in any form. But if with Paul one has an eschatology that sees a future for the body, sexual expression is seen in a different light. The body is not evil, and neither is it insignificant. Sexual expression has a purpose, a good purpose: to bring oneness in marriage. Outside this context, sexual expression cheapens the value of the body and is inconsistent with God's purpose for it.

The Gnostic could never have said, "Glorify God in your body." How could God be glorified by that which is evil?

But Paul's belief in the future of the body leads him to call for a life of responsibility in one's sexual life that will actually glorify God. The resurrection in the future makes a difference in the present.

Here again the not yet and the now come together.

Appendix to Chapter Eight

We cannot think about sex and marriage, on the one hand, and the Second Coming, on the other, without briefly considering another topic. We know that God will raise the body when Jesus returns, but what about sex and marriage after that point?

Most people who were reared as Adventists have probably thought at one point or another, ''I sure hope Jesus doesn't come until I get married, because there won't be any marriage in heaven.'' What can we say about the future in this regard?

The specific passages that seem to teach an end to marriage after the resurrection are Mark 12:18-27 and its parallels. The Sadducees, who did not believe in either resurrection or angels, tried to trap Jesus. They presented Him with a case that they believed made the whole idea of resurrection absurd. How would God possibly solve such a complex problem? Certainly, in light of the difficulties that such cases would produce, it would be best simply to put aside the whole idea of a resurrection. The story reads as follows:

> Then the Sadducees, who say there is no resurrection, came to him with a question. ''Teacher,'' they said, ''Moses wrote for us that if a man's brother dies and leaves a wife but no children, the man must marry the

widow and have children for his brother. Now there were seven brothers. The first one married and died without leaving any children. The second one married the widow, but he also died, leaving no child. It was the same with the third. In fact, none of the seven left any children. Last of all, the woman died too. At the resurrection whose wife will she be, since the seven were married to her?''

Jesus replied, ''Are you not in error because you do not know the Scriptures or the power of God? When the dead rise, they will neither marry nor be given in marriage; they will be like the angels in heaven. Now about the dead rising—have you not read in the book of Moses, in the account of the bush, how God said to him, 'I am the God of Abraham, the God of Isaac, and the God of Jacob'? He is not the God of the dead, but of the living. You are badly mistaken!''

Obviously, Jesus is not here giving a discourse about the new earth and the role that marriage will play in it. Rather, He is answering a trick question. As with many of Jesus' responses, at least some of the answer seems to reflect a degree of humor. Part of Jesus' answer is that those who are resurrected will be like angels. But remember, the Sadducees didn't believe in angels! I imagine onlookers must have smiled to hear Jesus solve part of their objection to one doctrine—the resurrection—by appealing to another doctrine—angels—in which they also did not believe.

Jesus goes on to tell them that they do not understand the power of God. In other words, God has ways of settling problems beyond our comprehension. The Sadducees limited God too much.

How, then, are we to interpret Jesus' words? Certainly, we should not ignore these words and concoct fanciful theories about the nature of marital life in heaven. Some in

Ellen White's day did just that, and she was quite emphatic in her advice to them.

> There are men today who express their belief that there will be marriages and births in the new earth; but those who believe the Scriptures cannot accept such doctrines. The doctrine that children will be born in the new earth is not a part of the "sure word of prophecy" (2 Peter 1:19). The words of Christ are too plain to be misunderstood. They should forever settle the question of marriages and births in the new earth. Neither those who shall be raised from the dead, nor those who shall be translated without seeing death, will marry or be given in marriage. They will be as the angels of God, members of the royal family.
>
> I would say to those who hold views contrary to this plain declaration of Christ, Upon such matters silence is eloquence. It is presumption to indulge in suppositions and theories regarding matters that God has not made known to us in His Word. We need not enter into speculation regarding our future state. . . .
>
> The Lord has made every provision for our happiness in the future life, but He has made no revelations regarding these plans, and we are not to speculate concerning them. Neither are we to measure the conditions of the future life by the conditions of this life.[3]

On the other hand, we should not make the mistake of speculating about what this absence of marriage actually entails. After all, not many of us have inside information about the marital or sexual life of angels! We do know that God is planning a home that we will enjoy. Even though it might be beyond our understanding, He will be able to work things out to everyone's satisfaction. And while we should avoid speculation, we certainly should not forget that it was God Himself who declared, "It is not good for man to be alone." He has hardly changed His mind, so we can look forward with confidence to that which He has in store for us.

Endnotes

[1] Jerome Murphy-O'Connor, "Corinthian Slogans in 1 Corinthians 6:12-20," *The Catholic Biblical Quarterly* 40 (1978):391-396.

[2] I have borrowed this phrase from my former professor, Leander E. Keck, *Paul and His Letters,* Proclamation Commentaries (Philadelphia: Fortress, 1979), pp. 108-111.

[3] *Selected Messages,* book 1, pp. 172, 173.

Chapter Nine

Eschatology and Political Ethics

During the twentieth century it has been hard to keep up with all the new theologies flooding the Christian world. Neo-Orthodox theology, existential theology, theology of hope, God is dead theology—the list goes on and on. One of the most popular recent theologies, especially in Latin America, has been liberation theology.[1]

According to liberation theology, the eschatological vision of Christianity is an end to oppression and the liberation of all people. But that vision concerns not only the future. People are being oppressed now. They need liberation now—here in this world. Christians are responsible to end oppression now. But how? Here various proponents of liberation theology differ, but some conclude that any means possible must be used, even violent revolution against tyranny. Some arm themselves not only with Bibles but also with machine guns and the tools of guerrilla warfare to move against the dictators and bring liberation to the poor and oppressed.

We certainly cannot deny that many people are oppressed and exploited. Does our eschatology help us know how to relate to oppression? I believe we receive help with this question from both ends of the New Testament.

In the first place, we have the example of Jesus. He lived at a time when God's people, of which He was a part, lived under the oppression of a foreign nation, Rome. Many Jews, including at least one of Jesus' disciples, believed that the answer was armed rebellion against Rome. These Zealots often lived in the country and robbed merchant trains to finance the future revolution. The history of the first century overflows with stories of would-be messiahs who (unsuccessfully) led groups against the Romans.

Yet Jesus rejected all this. He taught that Christians should turn the other cheek, go the second mile, and render to Caesar what is Caesar's (Matt. 5:39-41; Mark 12:17). He went quietly to His death, telling Pilate: "My kingdom is not of this world. If it were, my servants would fight to prevent my arrest by the Jews. But now my kingdom is from another place" (John 18:36).

Certainly in these words John sees significance not only for Jesus' day, but for his own time as well. Jesus' disciples do not fight because Jesus' kingdom is not of this world. Jesus destroys all illusions that the kingdom can be fully manifest in the political structures of this world. The kingdom cannot come by fighting or overturning one political structure in favor of another.

This does not mean that Jesus accepted the political structures of His day without criticism. Nor does it mean that He was not a threat to them. After all, He could call Herod "that fox," and He always spoke the truth about those in power.

It was more than the leaders of His day could endure. They crucified Him as a revolutionary. Yet He never for a moment accepted the Zealot answer to the problem of oppression. His kingdom went far beyond anything that could be realized merely in the political realm. Thus Jesus not only rejected violence for Himself; He declared that His followers do not fight because His kingdom is not of this world. In other words, the realization of the "not yet" aspect of eschatology has significance for political ethics. If the kingdom is beyond history and will be fully realized by

God's action, then it is inconsistent for Christ's followers to try to bring it now by fighting and violent revolution. Such means are not in keeping with the principles of the kingdom.

When John the revelator speaks about eschatology and the ethics of oppression in the last book of the Bible, he confirms this perspective. We can only understand his message, however, when we look at the book of Revelation from a broader perspective than we usually do. Thus some background material is in order here. (The following information in no way negates the traditional Adventist interpretation. It only adds an additional perspective from which to view it. It is a matter of "this ought you to have done and not left the other undone.")

We often think of the book of Revelation as written specifically for those who have lived from the mid-nineteenth century on. We need to recognize that the book was originally addressed to early Christian believers in seven specific cities in Asia Minor. When believers in Thyatira, for example, learned that there was a message for them from the exiled John and that it would be read during the Sabbath worship service, I imagine they came to church with lots of extra enthusiasm and expectancy. What would John say? They lived during difficult times. Demands were being placed on them by the state—totally unacceptable demands—demands that they bow down to statues and say, "Caesar is Lord." In addition, internal strife plagued the church. What would John say? Did he really have a message for them?

I seriously doubt that the people of these churches left disappointed from that special Sabbath service. We might think that they would have wondered about all those strange symbols. But we often forget that those symbols appear stranger to us than they did to first-century believers. The early Christians were used to reading a whole body of Jewish literature that employed such symbols to speak about the end of the world. Their past experience would have taught them to think about those symbols in relationship to their present experience as well as the promise of God's final victory.

Not only was there a body of Jewish literature with which they would have been familiar, but early Christians commonly applied eschatological symbols to their present experience.

We can find examples of this outside the book of Revelation. Take the symbol of antichrist, for instance. Only two books in the New Testament specifically mention this term, 1 and 2 John. We usually think of the antichrist as a single figure who rises up after the time of the early church and plays a significant role in the final events of earth's history. However, the picture in John's letters is quite different. In these letters John is addressing a specific problem. Certain early Christians had left the community of faith to which John belonged and had espoused the heresy known as Docetism. Those who believed in Docetism thought that the divine Christ did not really become human but only appeared to be human. Docetism was usually held by those who, like certain Corinthians we noted in the previous chapter, believed that all matter was evil. As John confronted this problem he used the symbol antichrist. Look at the following verses.

"Dear children, this is the last hour; and as you have heard that the antichrist is coming, even now many antichrists have come. This is how we know it is the last hour" (1 John 2:18).

"Who is the liar? It is the man who denies that Jesus is the Christ. Such a man is the antichrist—he denies the Father and the Son" (1 John 2:22).

"But every spirit that does not acknowledge Jesus is not from God. This is the spirit of the antichrist, which you have heard is coming and even now is already in the world" (1 John 4:3).

"Many deceivers, who do not acknowledge Jesus Christ as coming in the flesh, have gone out into the world. Any such person is the deceiver and the antichrist" (2 John 7).

Notice that while John is the only New Testament writer actually to use the term *antichrist,* obviously a tradition already predated him to the effect that in the last days an antichrist would come. John applied that expectation to his own time and declared that not only has one antichrist come but *many* have already come. They are those who refuse to accept that Jesus Christ came in the flesh. John sees this manifestation of antichrist as a sign of the end.

Such application of eschatological imagery to the present happened again and again among the early Christians, for certainly they saw themselves as living in the last days. This in no way, however, denies that these same symbols can have further application in our day at the end of time.

In the light of what we have seen, it is very hard to believe that those early Christians in a place like Thyatira would have failed to see the symbols of John's message as applying to their own day and situation, especially when John took pains to emphasize that the book was *not* sealed. On several occasions I have asked Adventist congregations to raise their hands if they believe John sealed up the book of Revelation to be understood only at the last day. The vast majority would inevitably raise their hands. But John says: "Then he told me, 'Do not seal up the words of the prophecy of this book, because the time is near' " (Rev. 22:10).

What sense, then, would the early Christian believers have made of Revelation? It is virtually certain that they would have seen the symbols of evil such as the beast and Babylon as referring to Rome, their present persecutor. After all, Christians had already used the name Babylon as a cryptic symbol for Rome. Peter, at the end of his first letter, sent greetings from those at Babylon (1 Peter 5:13) when he is almost certainly writing from Rome. And in Revelation 17:9 the readers learn that the beast's seven heads represent seven hills upon which the wicked woman sits. For years Rome had been known as the city of seven hills.

If the original readers of Revelation, then, understood these symbols as referring to Rome, the persecuting power under which they suffered, what message about the ethics of relating to an oppressive power would they have received?

First, Revelation would show them that the oppressive power did not operate on its own. It was empowered by the great dragon of Revelation 12, whom John explicitly identified as Satan. More is involved here than earthly politics. A cosmic struggle between Christ and Satan lies in the background.

Second, John was by no means afraid to speak out boldly about the evils of this power. There is no whitewash here. In Revelation 13 John showed how this power was persecuting the church. In chapter 17 he vividly portrayed her evils by calling her the mother of harlots, drunk with the blood of the saints and martyrs. John, through symbolic imagery, attacked the social evils of Rome. In this chapter he showed that when Babylon would fall, the merchants would mourn for her. He listed the commodities in which Rome dealt, and he ended by referring to the most abominable part of Rome's commerce — the selling of slaves. He then reminded his readers that these slaves were, after all, human beings. It is hard not to see strong social criticism in these words.

The merchants of the earth will weep and mourn over her because no one buys their cargoes any more — cargoes of gold, silver, precious stones and pearls; fine linen, purple, silk and scarlet cloth; every sort of citron wood, and articles of every kind made of ivory, costly wood, bronze, iron and marble; cargoes of cinnamon and spice, of incense, myrrh and frankincense, of wine and olive oil, of fine flour and wheat; cattle and sheep; horses and carriages; and bodies and souls of men. (Rev. 18:11-13).

And yet in spite of Rome's evil oppression and injustice, John never advocated that the people take up arms to overthrow her. He didn't advocate a violent revolution that relies on weapons of force. Instead, he gave advice consistent with the "already/not yet" aspects of eschatology that we have already surveyed.

John proclaimed the "already" aspect of the message by showing that Christ has already gained the victory. We see this message in Revelation 4 and 5 in the new song that the four living creatures and twenty-four elders sing: "And they sang a new song: 'You are worthy to take the scroll and to open its seals, because you were slain, and with your blood you purchased men for God from every tribe and language and people and nation. You have made them to be a kingdom and priests to serve our God, and they will reign on the earth' " (Rev. 5:9, 10). We see it again in Revelation 12, where we learn that Satan has been cast out and has but a short time, and the male child will rule with a rod of iron.

John proclaims the "not yet" aspect of eschatology by showing that even though the final results of this victory are not now visible on this earth, they soon will be, for Christ will return and His kingdom will fill the world. Justice, now so lacking in the world, will prevail.

All this meant that the oppressor had already been

defeated. While from a human perspective it might look as though Rome was the most powerful force in the world, John lifted the veil so his readers could see reality as it really is. Babylon had already fallen. Chapter 18 could already sing her funeral dirge. Rome may have looked powerful, but she was a sinking ship. Soon the hollowness of her power would stand revealed.

Such a message does not lead to ethical irresponsibility, as Jack T. Sanders claims. Instead, it encourages a realistic and courageous stance in the face of oppression. The Christian does not have to go out with guns and bombs to defeat the oppressive power; Christ has already defeated her. Christians, on the other hand, treat her as a defeated foe and refuse to give her the ultimate allegiance and worship she demands—allegiance and worship due only to God. Rather than violate the principles of God's kingdom, as revealed in the Sermon on the Mount, by taking up arms, Christians trust in Christ's victory, live in hope, and courageously resist the unholy demands, even unto death.

John's message not only brought wise admonition to the early Christians of Asia Minor; it gave them hope and comfort as well. God hadn't forgotten them. Christ had won the battle. Rome wouldn't have the last word. In fact, John even goes so far as to assure them that even if they are called on to die for their faith, their very death is a victory.

> The great dragon was hurled down—that ancient serpent called the devil or Satan, who leads the whole world astray. He was hurled to the earth, and his angels with him.
> Then I heard a loud voice in heaven say:
> "Now have come the salvation and the power and the kingdom of our God, and the authority of his Christ. For the accuser of our brothers, who accuses them before our

God day and night, has been hurled down. They over-
came him by the blood of the Lamb and by the word of
their testimony; they did not love their lives so much as
to shrink from death'' (Rev. 12:9-11).

When the early Christians saw their brothers or sisters
martyred, they were tempted to believe that Satan was
winning victory after victory. But John says ''no.'' They
have instead conquered Satan. For the first death, that
temporary sleep that is shattered by the resurrection, is the
strongest weapon Satan has. In the case of martyred
Christians, Satan has used his strongest weapon, and he has
still not been able to force Christians to give up their faith.
Thus Satan has not gained a victory. He has been conquered, for his most powerful weapon has been proved
ineffective in the face of true faith. The Christian martyrs,
by God's grace, had resisted.

Thus the Christians of Asia Minor received a message
that gave them the strength to resist the satanic power of
Rome. Far from making them ethically irresponsible, it
gave them strength to resist by a means much more
courageous than simply taking up the sword against Rome.
And not only was it courageous. It was consistent with the
principles of Christ's kingdom and the New Testament
message of eschatology.

The eschatological message of the New Testament frees
us from the folly of thinking that we can overthrow the
forces of oppression with our acts of violence. So often such
violent efforts have merely meant the exchange of one
tyrant for another. In 142 B.C. the Jews were overjoyed
when they were able to set up an independent kingdom with
their own ruler. They had defeated the Syrian oppressors.
Now justice would prevail. But before the end of the
century one of their *own* rulers would crucify 800 of his

political opponents, kill the wives and children of the victims in front of them, and look on while he banqueted and made love to his concubines. Christians are not called to overthrow the tyrant. God calls them, instead, to resist his blasphemous demands with courage in the full hope and assurance of Christ's completed victory and His promise for the future.

This distinction between "resisting," on the one hand, and violent revolt, on the other, is important.[2] While not engaging in violent revolt, Christians will resist the power of the political tyrant by refusing to give the demanded allegiance and by championing the cause of the oppressed. The book of Revelation leaves no room for an attitude that snuggles up as close as possible to the beast in order to make life easier. In fact, it clearly points to a time when there will be only two sides. All will stand either with the oppressors or with the oppressed. Those who have habitually failed to stand with the oppressed may find it difficult to know where to stand then, even if they think they understand all the prophecies.[3] You see, the New Testament also frees us from the folly of thinking that we can make peace with the oppressors and have them for our friends if we but ignore their oppression. Those very principles of the kingdom that keep us from violent revolution also impel us to be concerned not only for ourselves but for all the oppressed. This brings us to our next topic, "Eschatology and Social Ethics."

Endnotes

[1] For a representative anthology of writings by Latin-American liberation theologians, see Rosino Gibellini, ed., *Frontiers of Theology in Latin America,* trans. John Drury (Maryknoll, N.Y.: Orbis, 1975).

[2] When Jesus says "Do not resist evil" (or better, "the evil one") in the Sermon on the Mount (Matt. 5:39), He is certainly speaking in the latter sense.

[3] The same dragon of Revelation 12 stands behind all oppressive powers, and truly understanding the prophecies means recognizing the work of the dragon wherever it might be. According to Erwin Sicher, "Seventh-day Adventist Publications and the Nazi Temptation," *Spectrum*, Nov. 3, 1977, some Adventists in Germany had eyes to see the dragon at work in the papacy but were blind to his presence in the Nazi movement. Shouldn't we expect that even at the end a spiritual perception will be required that not only recognizes the evil of one organization but has eyes to see Satan's attempts to oppress and persecute whenever they may appear? Such perception comes only when one not only understands the literal significance of a prophecy but sees the basic principles that stand behind it.

Chapter Ten

Eschatology and Social Ethics

In his later writings Mark Twain became quite bitter about the Christian faith. However, in his bitterness he sometimes gave Christians something worth thinking about. For instance, he speaks of the inconsistencies in Christian thinking about heaven. He says of the Christian: "His heaven is like himself: strange, interesting, astonishing, grotesque. I give you my word, it has not a single feature in it that he *actually values*. It consists—utterly and entirely—of diversions which he cares next to nothing about, here in the earth, yet is quite sure he will like in heaven. Isn't it curious? Isn't it interesting? You must not think I am exaggerating, for it is not so. I will give you details." [1]

Twain goes on to give specific examples. One of these is the difference between the way people act toward each other here and now as compared with the way they think they will act then. In the following passage Twain uses some language that we would no longer use, but we can understand his purpose.

The inventor of their heaven empties into it all the nations of the earth, in one common jumble. All are on an equality absolute, no one of them ranking another; they have to be "brothers"; they have to mix together . . . there's no distinction. Here in the earth all nations hate each other, and every one of them hates the Jew. Yet every pious person adores that heaven and wants to get into it. He really does. And when he is in a holy rapture he thinks he thinks that if he were only there he would take all the populace to his heart, and hug, and hug, and hug, and hug!

He is a marvel—man is! I would I knew who invented him.[2]

Twain points out the utter inconsistency of hoping for one kind of a future world and yet living in a way that contradicts the hope. His point is well taken.

As Christians we hope for, speak about, and sing of a certain kind of future world. We say that we want to be part of that world. Even further, we believe that the future world has already broken into the present in the person of Jesus Christ. When we studied Jesus' teachings about the kingdom, especially in His parables, we saw that we can already begin to experience the kingdom if we are willing to trust Christ. This means that hoping for a future kingdom necessarily includes a commitment to the principles of that kingdom. Commitment makes a difference *now,* for how can we possibly be committed to the principles of God's kingdom without showing now that we accept and live by them?

The kingdom for which we hope is the kingdom of a God who shows no partiality. His incomprehensible love offers the blessing of salvation to anyone who will accept it. In His love He makes His kingdom a place where tears are wiped away; suffering and death are ended; poverty, disease, and hunger are abolished. Therefore, commitment to Christ's kingdom implies commitment to the destruction of pain, suffering, hunger, poverty, and even death.

Christians are realistic enough to know that all these enemies cannot be abolished before the return of Christ. But they also know that the kingdom can be anticipated in this world. People can be committed to its principles in this world. So Christians never simply sit back and wait for the Lord to come. That would be unthinkable. Because the kingdom already lives in the heart, Christians can't help acting now. God cares enough about His children to suffer when they suffer, to prepare a better world for them, and to open the veil so they can see the vision of that better world and find encouragement. How can people committed to His kingdom do less than work to relieve as much of that suffering as possible now?

Thus if one really understands eschatology, there can be no sharp dichotomy between the future vision and present action. Hoping for the kingdom can never make Christians indifferent toward their neighbors. Hoping for the kingdom means caring about the neighbors now, because that's what the kingdom is all about. Hoping for the kingdom isn't ticking off the days until a future event comes. Hoping for the kingdom is caring for and living for what the kingdom stands for.

No wonder Jesus ties our entrance into the future kingdom together with our concerns for our neighbor. Notice how eschatology and ethics come together in Jesus' familiar parable:

When the Son of Man comes in his glory, and all the angels with him, he will sit on his throne in heavenly glory. All the nations will be gathered before him, and he will separate the people one from another as a shepherd separates the sheep from the goats. He will put the sheep on his right and the goats on his left.

Then the King will say to those on his right, "Come, you who are blessed by my Father; take your inheritance, the kingdom prepared for you since the creation of the world. For I was hungry and you gave me something to

74

eat, I was thirsty and you gave me something to drink, I was a stranger and you invited me in, I needed clothes and you clothed me, I was sick and you looked after me, I was in prison and you came to visit me."

Then the righteous will answer him, "Lord, when did we see you hungry and feed you, or thirsty and give you something to drink? When did we see you a stranger and invite you in, or needing clothes and clothe you? When did we see you sick or in prison and go to visit you?"

The King will reply, "I tell you the truth, whatever you did for one of the least of these brothers of mine, you did for me."

Then he will say to those on his left, "Depart from me, you who are cursed, into the eternal fire prepared for the devil and his angels. For I was hungry and you gave me nothing to eat, I was thirsty and you gave me nothing to drink, I was a stranger and you did not invite me in, I needed clothes and you did not clothe me, I was sick and in prison and you did not look after me."

They also will answer, "Lord, when did we see you hungry or thirsty or a stranger or needing clothes or sick or in prison, and did not help you?"

He will reply, "I tell you the truth, whatever you did not do for one of the least of these, you did not do for me."

Then they will go away to eternal punishment, but the righteous to eternal life (Matt. 25:31-46).

Interpreters of this parable find certain difficulties in it, so it is not surprising that several different interpretations have been given.

Some have taken it as a statement about the basis of judgment for everyone. God will judge on the basis of how we have treated our neighbors. If we have done good things, we will be admitted; if not, we will be excluded. This sounds very much like salvation by works, however. So other scholars have come up with different interpretations.

Some have noticed the word *nations* in verse 32. It translates the same Greek word often rendered "Gentile." They suggest that this parable is only talking about the Gentiles who have not heard the gospel. Since these Gentiles have not had an opportunity to respond to the message of righteousness by faith, God judges them by a different standard. Therefore the parable doesn't contradict salvation by faith, but gives an alternative standard for unbelievers.

Other scholars, many of whom are uncomfortable with the notion that some people might be saved apart from hearing the gospel, point to the parallel between this passage and Matthew 10:40-42. Here they see a key to its interpretation. In Matthew 10 Jesus instructs His disciples and sends them out on a missionary journey. He concludes: "He who receives you receives me, and he who receives me receives the one who sent me. Anyone who receives a prophet because he is a prophet will receive a prophet's reward, and anyone who receives a righteous man because he is a righteous man will receive a righteous man's reward. And if anyone gives a cup of cold water to one of these little ones because he is my disciple, I tell you the truth, he will certainly not lose his reward" (Matt. 10:40-42).

These interpreters tie the "little ones," who are Christ's missionaries in Matthew 10, with the "least of these my brethren" in Matthew 25. They conclude, therefore, that Christ was talking about how His missionaries are treated in the latter passage as well. He was not saying that all those who are kind to their neighbors will enter the kingdom, but that whoever receives with kindness the Christian missionary, who brings the gospel, will enter the kingdom. The basis of salvation is always the same: reception of the gospel. Here Christ warned against ignoring or rejecting the Christian missionary, who not only brought the good news of salvation, but also was dependent on the hospitality of those who heard.

Actually, each interpretation has problems. Certain elements in the parable hardly seem to fit with the last interpretation. It is true that early Christian missionaries depended on the hospitality of those to whom they preached, but it is hard to imagine people going around visiting sick missionaries. Besides, the people in the parable seem to have been unaware of their actions. On the other hand, using the basis of one word to limit the parable's application to only those who have never heard the gospel is hardly careful interpretation.

How, then, do we relate this parable to the message of salvation by grace through faith? I believe Jesus did not intend for this parable to be a final statement on the basis for judgment. His concern here was more with the fruits of salvation than how to obtain salvation. He wanted to show the values, concerns, and actions that will characterize those who have set their minds on the kingdom. There is a connection between the promise and the present. Our fitness for the future kingdom *is* necessarily related to our present attitude toward the principles of the kingdom.

This does not mean that salvation comes by works. In fact, only those who have been justified by God's grace are free to end their attempts at self-justification. Every such attempt is part of our natural state and keeps us from reaching out to our neighbors. Only those who have accepted God's grace can appreciate what the kingdom is all about.

Thus, to shut our eyes to the needs of others with a glib

"That will all be taken care of when Jesus comes" would prostitute New Testament eschatology. As John tells us: "He who does not love abides in death" (1 John 3:14, RSV). But those who love are already bringing a taste of the kingdom to the world.

Paul too, in his doctrine of righteousness by faith, clearly reveals this connection between grace and love for the neighbor. God's grace means that God shows no partiality. If God embraces all humans as His children, it is a denial of God to reject any human through prejudiced distinctions. Thus it is no accident that the significant discussion of salvation by faith in Galatians 2 and 3 ends with the great statement of oneness in Christ. Oneness and love for others are intrinsic to Paul's message of salvation by grace.

Unfortunately, this social, ethical dimension often ends up on the short end of Adventist discussions about salvation. Both "perfectionists" and advocates of "justification by faith" tend to focus exclusively on the personal question How can I be saved? All too many of us fail to give adequate attention to the social dimension of salvation. Attempts to emphasize the social dimension we sometimes quickly label as "social gospel." So we therefore write off these suggestions without giving them serious consideration.

I do not mean that there is some specific social program that the church must get involved in, or that Christian social concern must always take the same shape. Specific ways of helping one's neighbor will differ from person to person and culture to culture. But genuine hope for the coming kingdom cannot exist without social concern for the present needs of God's children. Although our primary task is to preach the gospel, a concern for others that focuses only on the spiritual while ignoring the physical and social needs can only pervert the gospel of love. Far from dulling social concern and responsibility, a genuine understanding of eschatology will lead to a realization in our lives of these words of John: "We know that we have passed from death to life, because we love our brothers. Anyone who does not love remains in death" (1 John 3:14).

Ellen White's attitude toward the abolition of slavery provides an excellent example of social concern. Some believers in her day felt that Christians could never make progress in this area and shouldn't even waste their time trying. Some considered as useless even the simple act of voting to abolish slavery. One pioneer argued:

> We say we bid all reforms, Godspeed! but some are laboring for reforms which they will never see accomplished. As much as anyone, from our very soul we detest and abhor that foul blot on our country—slavery! And our sympathies are with those whose hearts burn with the love of freedom, and who would desire to see the bondman loosed from his chains. But he who expects to see the land freed entirely from this curse, or even to see slavery contentedly confine itself within certain limits, we can but regard as laboring under a false hope; for the character which prophetic pencil has given to the two-horned beast (Revelation 13:11), a symbol of our country, is that he shall speak as a dragon! [3]

Another, while arguing against voting, said:

> "But you can vote against slavery," says one. Very well; supposing I do, what will be the effect? In the last great persecution, which is just before us, the decrees of the image will be against the "bond" as well as the free. Bondmen will exist then until the last—till God interposes to deliver His saints, whether bond or free. My

vote then cannot free the slaves; and all apparent progress toward emancipation will only exasperate their master, and cause an aggravation of those evils that it was intended to cure. I cannot, therefore, vote against slavery, neither can I vote for it.'' [4]

But Ellen White had a very different attitude. She spoke out against slavery.

God is punishing this nation for the high crime of slavery. He has the destiny of the nation in His hands. He will punish the South for the sin of slavery, and the North for so long suffering its overreaching and overbearing influence.

At the Conference at Roosevelt, New York, August 3, 1861, when the brethren and sisters were assembled on the day set apart for humiliation, fasting, and prayer, the Spirit of the Lord rested upon us, and I was taken off in vision and shown the sin of slavery, which has so long been a curse to this nation. The fugitive slave law was calculated to crush out of man every noble, generous feeling of sympathy that should arise in his heart for the oppressed and suffering slave. It was in direct opposition to the teaching of Christ. God's scourge is now upon the North, because they have so long submitted to the advances of the slave power. The sin of Northern proslavery men is great. They have strengthened the South in their sin by sanctioning the extension of slavery; they have acted a prominent part in bringing the nation into its present distressed condition. [5]

Ellen White didn't think that it was enough to say, ''When Jesus comes, He will free the slaves.'' She looked for a kingdom where God would free the slaves, but that vision of the promise motivated her to action in the present. If freedom was a principle of the kingdom, she would live for it and work for it now. And with her strong speeches she certainly did work for the abolition of slavery.

In the previous chapter we saw the futility of trying to usher in the kingdom by violently overthrowing political structures, no matter how violent and oppressive they might be. But we live in a society where we have unprecedented opportunity to influence the course of events. Every time we vote, every time we choose how to spend our time and money, we have an opportunity to ask how our actions will contribute to our needy neighbor and further the principles of God's kingdom. Our attention has a dual focus: a vision of the future and a present work to be done.

In a sense, the building in which I work points out the dual focus in our Adventist history. It was built in 1892— a time when many Adventists just knew that the Second Coming was very near. Yet Adventists in the Pacific Northwest recognized a work to be done in the area of Christian education. They forged ahead and gave no thought to doing the work halfway because the Lord was about to come. They constructed a building much larger than would have been necessary for their present needs. And they not only built it large; they built it well. (Some of us who have offices in it are tempted to wish that they hadn't built it so well. If it had fallen down years ago, we might now enjoy more modern quarters.) The building still stands as testimony to the fact that Christians with a vivid vision of the future promise can still act responsibly in the present, contributing to the betterment of this world while hoping for the next.

Endnotes

[1] Mark Twain, *Letters From the Earth,* ed. Bernard DeVoto (Greenwich, Conn.: Fawcett Crest, 1962), p. 16.

[2] *Ibid.,* p. 19.

[3] "True Reforms and Reformers," *Review and Herald,* June 26, 1856, p. 68. (This editorial is unsigned and is presumably by Uriah Smith.)

[4] R. F. Cottrell, "How Shall I Vote?" *Review and Herald,* Oct. 30, 1856, p. 205.

[5] *Testimonies,* vol. 1, p. 264.

Chapter Eleven

The Wedding

One night several years ago my wife and I were awakened when we heard the neighbor, a volunteer fireman, jump into his car and race out the driveway. Moments later the town fire alarm went off. We got up to see what was happening and noticed clouds of smoke billowing from the college campus where I teach. Naturally, the fire concerned us, and we wanted to check out the situation; but the children were still asleep, and we didn't really want to get them up or leave them by themselves.

Finally I volunteered to stay with the kids, since my wife was quite curious. She drove off in our Chevrolet and promised to return quickly with a report.

After she left, the smoke turned into great balls of flame. Although I couldn't tell what was on fire (it turned out to be the old campus auditorium), I feared that it was the administration building, which contained not only my office but also my books, files, and class notes. I got impatient and decided to ride my bike down the street toward the campus to a point where I could get a good view of the building. No sooner had I started, however, when a car turned the corner down at the end of the street. It was coming from the direction of the campus. I concluded from the lights that it was a Chevrolet, and assuming that it was my wife, I turned around and headed back to the house to meet her.

I turned out to be right and wrong. It was a Chevrolet, but

it wasn't my wife. It was a policeman. Since the fire was obviously the work of an arsonist, he was looking for suspicious-looking people. And someone riding a bicycle at 2:00 a.m., going in the opposite direction of the fire, did look suspicious!

Before I knew it, his lights were flashing and I was at the side of the street while he plied me with questions. I told him the perfectly logical story I have just related, but it didn't seem to convince him. He kept saying things like "Your wife, huh? Do I look like your wife?" I began to get worried when he called for assistance from another unit. Soon another police car arrived, lights flashing, and screeched to a halt. The policeman jumped out, and I saw that it was a friend of mine. In fact, he was taking a class from me at the time. It was two days before an exam, and he didn't want my ordeal to continue any longer than necessary. I was off the hook. It really felt great to have a friend come to the rescue.

Adventists believe that our true Friend and Brother, Jesus Christ, is coming to rescue us from the destructiveness of sin. We refer to this as the "blessed hope." Repeatedly in the previous chapters we have spoken of Christians as those who hope for the Second Coming. We have argued that hope in the promise motivates us in the present. But there is one final problem. What if the promise isn't a hope at all?

The first time I taught a college Bible class, I left a few minutes at the end of the semester for students to talk about anything they wanted to. I passed out paper and had them write down topics that concerned them. It didn't matter whether or not the questions had anything to do with the class. Three topics topped the list. Two I had expected, but one surprised me.

In third place was a subject of the educational environment. "Why do we have to do this?" "Why can't we do that?'' I had expected such questions. In the second place came questions about sex, dating, marriage, etc. Those too I had expected. But far above either of these issues, in first place, were questions about the Second Coming. That surprised me, although I guess it shouldn't have. After all, we are the people of the ''blessed hope.''

But as I read the questions, they didn't sound very much like they had anything to do with hope. Anxiety and concern were more like it. There were questions like: ''How bad will the time of trouble really be?'' ''How will we know when to flee for the mountains?'' ''What is the last sign before the close of probation?'' ''Are the problems in the Middle East signs that time is very short?'' They don't sound much like hope, do they?

Sometimes the images of Scripture can be especially helpful in not only providing us with information but also in helping us catch the attitudes and emotions that are also part of God's communication to us. We need especially to remember one of the images God uses for the Second Coming in Revelation. The revelator compares the Second Coming to a wedding. We are the bride; Jesus is the groom.

Then I heard what sounded like a great multitude, like the roar of rushing waters and like loud peals of thunder, shouting: ''Hallelujah! For our Lord God Almighty reigns. Let us rejoice and be glad and give him glory! For the wedding of the Lamb has come, and his bride has made herself ready. Fine linen, bright and clean, was given her to wear.'' (Fine linen stands for the righteous acts of the saints.)

Then the angel said to me, ''Write: 'Blessed are those who are invited to the wedding supper of the Lamb!' '' And he added, ''These are the true words of God'' (Rev. 19:6-9).

I have noticed a couple of things about weddings. They are happy occasions, and people look forward to them. On a college campus a number of announcements are made come spring. Dates are set. Sometimes when I see one of the newly engaged girls, I ask, "How many days is it?" Somehow she always seems to know what I am talking about. She never stares at me and asks, "How many days till what?" She also inevitably knows how many days it is. It's right on the tip of her tongue: "Sixty-five days" or whatever. And you know, I've never had a girl say, "Well, it's 65 days, but I sure wish it were five years."

If the Second Coming is something like a wedding, why don't we who believe in it share more of the joy and eager anticipation of a bride? I think there are several reasons.

First, we are not completely sure about the One who is coming. We aren't sure we can trust Him. His justice seems so severe. I'm sure a bride wouldn't look forward to her wedding very much if she thought her new husband would beat her every night.

But in our case such fears are totally unfounded. Notice what Ellen White says about our misunderstanding of God's character:

> God has bound our hearts to Him by unnumbered tokens in heaven and in earth. Through the things of nature, and the deepest and tenderest earthly ties that human hearts can know, He has sought to reveal Himself to us. Yet these but imperfectly represent His love. Though all these evidences have been given, the enemy of good blinded the minds of men, so that they looked upon God with fear; they thought of Him as severe and unforgiving. Satan led men to conceive of God as a being whose chief attribute is stern justice—one who is a severe judge, a harsh, exacting creditor. He pictured the Creator

as a being who is watching with jealous eye to discern the errors and mistakes of men, that He may visit judgments upon them. It was to remove this dark shadow, by revealing to the world the infinite love of God, that Jesus came to live among men.[1]

Once the dark shadow has been removed and we see what God has done for us in Christ, we can look forward to being with such a God.

Second, we are unsure about our own preparation. Maybe God will find one defect of character. After all, Revelation 19:7, 8 says that the "bride has made herself ready" and had on "fine linen." It also says that this fine linen represents the righteous deeds of the saints. What if my deeds don't seem to have been all that righteous?

But notice that our text says also that the bride was given the fine linen. Her preparation was a gift from the groom. When I was visiting Mexico, I discovered that it is traditional there for the groom to provide the bride with her wedding dress. What a fitting symbol of God's grace! Again, beautiful words from Ellen White give us confidence.

> We should not make self the center, and indulge anxiety and fear as to whether we shall be saved. All this turns the soul away from the Source of our strength. Commit the keeping of your soul to God, and trust in Him. Talk and think of Jesus. Let self be lost in Him. Put away all doubt; dismiss your fears. Say with the apostle Paul, "I live; yet not I, but Christ liveth in me: and the life which I now live in the flesh I live by the faith of the Son of God, who loved me, and gave himself for me." Galatians 2:20. Rest in God. He is able to keep that which you have committed to Him. If you will leave

yourself in His hands, He will bring you off more than conqueror through Him that has loved you.

When Christ took human nature upon Him, He bound humanity to Himself by a tie of love that can never be broken by any power save the choice of man himself. Satan will constantly present allurements to induce us to break this tie—to choose to separate ourselves from Christ. Here is where we need to watch, to strive, to pray, that nothing may entice us to choose another master; for we are always free to do this. But let us keep our eyes fixed upon Christ, and He will preserve us. Looking unto Jesus, we are safe. Nothing can pluck us out of His hand.[2]

Finally, too often we focus our attention on the events that occur before the Second Coming instead of on the One who comes and the new kingdom He has prepared for us. It's true that things on this earth will get worse before the Second Coming, but we have the promise that God will be with us. Besides, all this is nothing compared with the joy of being with God in our new home.

Can you imagine a bride-to-be who couldn't talk or even think about the groom, the wedding, or the new home, but instead was consumed with the thought that before she got married she would have to go to a physician and get a blood test! He would stick a needle in her arm and take out blood! What a terrifying thought! Such an attitude would appear very strange. Clearly, the Second Coming can be a hope only when we place our attention not on those preliminary events but on the groom and our new home with Him.

When we grasp the good news about the "already" eschatological message—who Jesus is and what He has done for us—the "not yet" will become joyful anticipation. Then, as we have seen, joyous hope in the promise will make a difference in the present. New values will motivate our actions so that our lives may become consistent with our vision of the promise. This is the real message of eschatology.

Several years ago my sister was staying with us while she was planning her wedding. It was fun to see her joyful excitement as she made plans. One night my wife and I went to bed while she was still out shopping. In what seemed like the middle of the night, we heard a knock on the bedroom door. On the other side my sister asked, "Are you awake?" We turned over, and I answered, "I guess we are now!" then asked what she wanted. "I want to show you something," she replied.

We invited her in, and she excitedly showed us what she had selected that night—a knife, a fork, and a spoon. I don't know about you, but I have a hard time getting excited about knives and forks and spoons, especially in the middle of the night. But for her this was very exciting. It was part of the new home for which she was planning. All of her thoughts seemed to be on that new home.

A few nights later we heard another knock on the door, this time even later than before. Again we invited my sister in. She reached around the corner and flicked on the light. Do you know how terrible it is to have a bright light shining in your eyes after you've been asleep? But when she came in the door, the light on the ceiling was nothing compared with her face. "Look what I bought today," she exulted, and danced in with a beautiful, flowing white wedding gown.

That's the kind of joy we should have as we look forward to the promise. "Let us rejoice and be glad and give him glory! For the wedding of the Lamb has come, and his bride has made herself ready" (Rev. 19:7).

Endnotes

[1] *Steps to Christ*, pp. 10, 11.

[2] *Ibid.*, pp. 71, 72.